the little book of
SELF-CARE

Hardie Grant

QUADRILLE

Self-care

Definition:
noun

1. The practice of taking action to preserve or improve one's own health.

2. The practice of taking an active role in protecting one's own wellbeing and happiness, in particular during periods of stress.

It matters because...

- Everyone is unique and deserves to be cherished.

- Feeling wrung out all the time is no way to live life.

- Mental, emotional and physical health are worth taking care over.

- It provides a foundation to care for others.

- They haven't yet invented the full body transplant.

- Hey, who needs an excuse?

Sleep

Eat

Listen

Forgive

Chat

Accept

Relax

Exercise

Think about it

Self-care is an act of **self-respect.**

Ditch the guilt

Understand that putting yourself first is not a luxury but a necessity, and is fundamental to happier moods and reduced stress and anxiety.

Self-care takes practice – having a bubble bath, once, does not count.

Think of self-care in terms of airline safety. You have to put on the oxygen mask first before being able to help others.

Five ways to wellbeing

Connect: talk and listen, be there, feel connected

Give: your time, your words, your presence

Take notice: remember the simple things that give you joy

Keep learning: embrace new experiences, see opportunities, surprise yourself

Be active: do what you can, enjoy what you do, move your mood

MIND
mental health charity

The body achieves that which the mind believes.

Exercise for the mind

Caring fully for yourself can be best achieved by living according to your values.

Pin down your current values and keep them front of mind in all that you do...

1. When were you happiest?

2. When were you most proud?

3. When were you most fulfilled?

4. Why were each of these moments memorable and important to you?

5. Based on your experiences of happiness, pride and fulfilment, think about what it is that you value.

6. Make choices based on these values.

Live the life that is right for you

Learning to cut out the clamour and expectations that society has for you is an imperative element of self-care. No one can live well according to the demands of others.

Try to concentrate solely on
what motivates you in life.

Self-care: the basics #1

Never put off visiting a doctor, attend all screenings you are invited to (no, not films) and *always* follow up on medical care.

Think about self-care as part of your lifestyle. Do not be misled into thinking of it as just another trend. It is simply about understanding yourself and your needs, and committing to fitting this into your life, without feeling guilty.

If you want to be a light for others,
you have to glow yourself.

But I'm too busy...

In order to begin a new routine involving self-care, a change of mind-set must be made.

Self-care is as important as arriving to work on time or making the children's packed lunches. If you have time to check social media feeds, you have time to look after yourself.

Avoid...

- Spending 30 minutes scrolling through social media
- Drowning in box sets
- Wasting time on email ping-pong
- Being interrupted by notifications

Try...

- Meeting a friend
- Hosting a dinner party
- Talking to family
- Doing a digital detox

Once you've decided to prioritize self-care, guard your time as if it's the most valuable jewel in the world. It is your time and it is **precious**.

"Learn to enjoy every minute of your life. Be happy now. Don't wait for something outside of yourself to make you happy in the future. Think how really precious is the time you have to spend, whether it's at work or with your family. Every minute should be enjoyed and savoured."

EARL NIGHTINGALE

Whether it's a relaxing or fun activity, ask yourself what you need to do every week to enhance yourself.

Be imaginative and bold in your choice of activities.

Look at the bigger picture

Don't hesitate about articulating the dreams you've put on the back burner. Think in terms of the months and years ahead. Perhaps you'd like to take up horse riding or learn how to play a musical instrument?

Write down your lifelong ambitions and plan how these can become practically and financially viable.

Getting the big stuff right

In addition to keeping doctor, dentist and optician appointments, conduct regular life audits about yourself, your partner, where you live, your career, your passions and what more you want to achieve.

Ask yourself: how am I doing?

Five small steps:

1. Decide which areas of your life to examine: health, relationships, finance, spirituality.

2. Write down questions to ask yourself: Am I happy? Am I using my full potential?

3. Answer honestly.

4. Create a practical plan to address any issues.

5. Set yourself a time limit – it could take an hour, a month or five years to achieve what you desire.

Take a break

Getting away every now and then, even if you're not particularly stressed, can help you disconnect and relax.

A romantic night away with your partner? A weekend going wild with friends? A trip to an exotic destination you've always hoped to visit? All three and more? These trips are not going to book themselves; dynamically take steps to begin such journeys.

"We don't receive wisdom; we must discover it for ourselves after a journey that no one can take for us..."

MARCEL PROUST

The art of simplification

Look at all aspects of your life
and ask yourself which elements
can be discarded. Decluttering
will allow you more time to
discover what it is you want
and will help you to take life
in a direction of your choosing...

- Delete
- Cancel
- Recycle
- Unsubscribe

Never regret spending money on items and experiences that enhance your every day...

- An excellent haircut
- A lovely winter coat
- Direct flights
- A functioning phone
- Comfortable underwear

Remember

Once you have worked out what it is that makes you feel happy... go for it.

Look after yourself. **You deserve it.**

Open your eyes

Brutal as it may sound, setting your alarm 15 minutes earlier than usual can set you on course for a tranquil, controlled day. Enjoy a cup of tea, stretch, meditate or just sit quietly and think about what lies before you. Those precious minutes spent alone may well become the most valuable time of the day.

"The eye is the lamp of the body. So, if your eye is healthy your whole body will be full of light."

MATTHEW
Chapter 2, Verses 22–23

The world is beautiful outside
when there is stability inside.

Meditation can reduce the symptoms of anxiety, stress and insomnia, and lower blood pressure. And frankly, what's not to like about taking 10 minutes a day to be with yourself in a state of calm?

It's time to sit down, close your eyes and seek inner peace.

Ommm...

Zzz

To care fully for yourself is
to care seriously about good
sleeping habits.

Sleeping well is one of the
cornerstones to achieving a
healthy mind and body. Cells
repair themselves during sleep,
thoughts are ordered, worries
settled and the body rejuvenated.

Five benefits of a good night's sleep

1. Mood – plenty of rest can put you in a positive headspace

2. Concentration – increased energy levels help sharpen attention

3. Stress levels – feeling bright-eyed and bushy-tailed can reduce tension

4. Perspective – it is much easier to see things clearly when you're feeling fresh

5. Health – a boosted immune system can help keep your body safe

Power nap

Find a time to kick back, relax and recharge at home.

Consistency is key

A regular bedtime will help you to wind down at the end of the day. Drifting off is much easier when your body knows the routine.

Eyes are universally acknowledged to be the windows to the soul. Therefore, give their decoration due care.

Still haven't mastered the perfect winged cat eye? Watch these magnificent YouTube vloggers for makeup masterclasses...

Chloe Morello: Australian makeup artist works miracles with bold eye colour.

Michelle Phan: American makeup artist who has notched up over one billion views. If anyone can help you master liquid eyeliner, it's Michelle.

Alissa Ashley: Former cosmetics retailer Alissa Ashley's tutorial on fixing cosmetics mistakes is gold.

"The beauty of a woman must be seen from in her eyes, because that is the doorway to her heart, the place where love resides."

AUDREY HEPBURN

10 meditation apps

1. #SelfCare
2. Calm
3. Headspace
4. Stop, Breathe and Think
5. Buddhify
6. Omvana
7. Breathe
8. Breethe: Sleep & Meditation
9. Smiling Mind
10. Simple Habit – Meditation

Top tips for healthy eyes

- Wear sunglasses.

- Visit the optician.

- Eat a wide variety of fruit and vegetables including lots of dark leafy greens.

- Avoid smoking – it really is the worst thing for eye health (and, let's be honest, health in general).

Self-care: the basics #2

For healthy screen use:

- Apply the 20-20-20 rule. Every 20 minutes look at something 20 feet away for 20 seconds. That will give your eye muscles a rest.

- Try to blink regularly. Focusing on a screen could make you blink less, which may make your eyes dry and uncomfortable.

- Don't sit too close to your screen. Keep it in a position that is slightly tilted away from you.

THE COLLEGE OF OPTOMETRISTS

Being positive isn't pretending everything is good, it's seeing the good in everything.

" *He who can no longer pause to wander and stand rapt in awe, is as good as dead; his eyes are closed.* "

ALBERT EINSTEIN

The world around you

Allow yourself to be moved by small beauties. Find a feather or a flower and look closely; it's all in the details.

Take time to look up. There is always more to see above – beautiful ceilings, cloud formations and more.

"Rest is not idleness, and to lie sometimes on the grass under trees on a summer's day, listening to the murmur of the water, or watching the clouds float across the sky, is by no means a waste of time."

JOHN LUBBOCK

Tidy house, tidy mind

The more you care for your immediate surroundings, the more they will care for you. You will find yourself smiling at a well-ordered bookshelf or a riotous display of cushions.

"If you haven't cried, your eyes can't be beautiful."

SOPHIA LOREN

It's easy to fall into the trap of thinking that self-care is a vastly complicated operation involving fitness apps, macrobiotic diets and expensive unguents. Instead, the foundations are free and easy – it just requires the formulation of good habits.

Self-care: the basics #3

Each adult needs between six (for older people) and nine hours of sleep a night. For a good night's sleep, every night remember to:

1. Go to bed at a regular time.

2. Avoid screens an hour before bed.

3. Have some downtime by enjoying a warm bath or reading a book.

Speak kindly to yourself

Look at yourself in the mirror and say at least one affirming comment out loud. The power of the spoken word is such that articulating positive thoughts lifts your mood and provides the confidence to turn away from the mirror believing in yourself.

Speak of yourself as you
would someone you love.

"Wear a smile and have friends,
wear a scowl and have wrinkles."

GEORGE ELIOT

Self-care: the basics #4

Smiling is a sure-fire way to bring yourself little bursts of joy. Greet those people you see every day with a smile and watch as it is returned. Investing in these casual acquaintances makes you more empathetic and less lonely.

Buy a red lipstick

Nothing says power and glamour like red lipstick, so it's no surprise that during financial recessions, sales of red lipstick rocket. The small tube of red opulence is the most cost-efficient method of instantly lifting any outfit, face or mood.

Five iconic red lipsticks:

- M.A.C's Ruby Woo
- Chanel's Pirate
- Revlon's Fire and Ice
- Dior's 999
- YSL's Le Rouge

If you can't say anything nice,
don't say anything at all.

"Wrinkles should merely indicate where smiles have been."

MARK TWAIN

"Always laugh when you can, it is cheap medicine."

LORD BYRON

When to say no

Shedding unnecessary obligations can be the key to unlocking more time. With time comes freedom and with freedom comes the opportunity to do what you want, or need, at a moment of your choosing.

Golden rules for good eating habits

Variety
Eat food of different cultures, textures, colours and flavours.

Moderation
No food is "bad", but remember to eat treats in moderation.

Go fresh
Try to cook with fresh ingredients from scratch. If this is too complicated, consider a recipe box scheme, which does the recipe planning for you.

Good food = good mood

The human tongue has up to 8,000 taste buds. Make it your business to get them working. If you find yourself eating or cooking the same limited repertoire, try to fire up all your taste buds by eating foods way off your usual palate.

Good sources of iron

- Liver
- Soya bean flour
- Watercress

Good sources of vitamin C

- Oranges

- Strawberries

- Potatoes

Good sources of vitamin D

- Herring
- Egg yolks
- Fortified breakfast cereals

Good sources of calcium

- Okra
- Tofu
- Cheese

The swedish art of *fika*

Fika is the art of taking a coffee with friends. The daily ritual of *fika* is all about slowing down and connecting with the people you care about.

Come on, let's *fika*.

Cheers to that

As with all of life's great pleasures, alcoholic drinks should be drunk to give pleasure, not to cause pain later. Here's a reminder of the benefits of drinking less:

- More energy
- Better skin
- Fewer hangovers...

Hydration is key

We should be drinking about 2 litres of water a day. Here are three ways to keep your drinks interesting:

1. Add slices of cucumber, lemon, lime and mint.

2. Add sparkling water to half a glass of ordinary water for a mildly fizzy experience.

3. Add cubes of frozen fresh fruit juice.

Everyone is different. We all have different urges and cravings. Feed your hunger in a way that suits you:

Explore different sorts of exercise until you find one that makes you feel alive.

So many cultural offerings are free and accessible. Branch out and experience culture that is outside your comfort zone.

Delve deeper into the big questions of life. Read religious literature and visit your local church, mosque, synagogue, chapel or temple.

Ask questions.

Breathing is your greatest friend.
Return to it in all your troubles and
you will find comfort and guidance...

Relax

- Breathe through your nose to filter out irritants.

- Use your diaphragm and take deep breaths to fully oxygenate your body.

- Exhale gently.

- And repeat...

A few minutes of calm

Standing up, sitting or lying down, try this calming breathing technique:

- Try breathing in through your nose and out through your mouth.

- Let your breath flow as deep down into your belly as is comfortable, without forcing it.

- Breathe in gently and regularly. Some people find it helpful to count steadily from 1–5. You may not be able to reach 5 at first.

- Then, without pausing or holding your breath, let it flow out gently, counting from 1–5 again, if you find this helpful.

- Keep doing this for 3–5 minutes.

UK NATIONAL HEALTH SERVICE

The power of scent

More than all the other senses, smell is closely linked to memory and can be utilized to instantly relive an emotion – something to remember when you're feeling nostalgic.

Refreshing and rejuvenating scents

- Bake vanilla pods in the oven for an instant homely aroma.

- Spritz your pillow with lavender water to create a calming atmosphere.

- Fill your house/office with scented plants such as jasmine or eucalyptus.

- Throw open the doors and windows for some fresh air.

- Pour coffee beans into a jar and leave unopened for an easy air-freshener.

Listen up

Your body hears everything your mind tells it – stay positive.

Pump up the volume

Changing the sheets? Doing the laundry? Making dinner? Choose your favourite tracks, sing along while you are working and, with the help of the music, turn mundane tasks into the best of times.

"*Music is a moral law. It gives soul to the universe, wings to the mind, flight to the imagination, and charm and gaiety to life and to everything.*"

PLATO

How to get in the zone and stay there

When you really need to concentrate on a task, listen to video game music. Designed especially to keep players involved in a singular task for long periods of time, video game music is easy to listen to but not overbearing.

Modern life is such that music is everywhere, in our ears as we commute, in the background in shops, on headphones as we exercise. Music can pierce the heart and move people in ways that are mysterious and magical, so treat yourself to enjoying it properly.

Used wisely, music can be a powerful tool. Take time to listen and appreciate music as an activity on its own.

Walk to your local park, find a comfortable spot and listen to your favourite tracks.

"Music makes us want to live."

MARY J. BLIGE

Mute the hate

- Report hateful messages on social media.

- Unfollow people who are unkind to others.

- Don't engage in online slanging matches.

Every year WQXR, New York's classical music radio station, asks its listeners for their favourite classical pieces of music. Give your ears, and indeed your entire being, a treat and listen to those recommended in its most recent poll:

1. Beethoven: Symphony No. 9, "Choral"

2. Dvorak: Symphony No. 9, "From the New World"

3. Beethoven: Symphony No. 7

4. Beethoven: Symphony No. 5

5. Mahler: Symphony No. 2, "Resurrection"

Silent contemplation can:

- Harmonize your mind and body.
- Help you tap into your inner wisdom.
- Give you a chance to remember.
- Teach you the value of words.
- Improve your awareness.

Unplug from the constant pings of modern life. Choose a time of the day when you want solitude and peace, and put all devices on aeroplane mode.

Mindful listening:

1. Don't interrupt.

2. Pause before you respond.

3. Ask if you don't understand what has been said.

4. Repeat what has been said in your own words.

5. Encourage the other person to tell you more.

Listen up

Get to know yourself by paying attention to your thoughts and feelings:

- What keeps you up at night?

- What is your body trying to tell you?

- Are you working too much?

- Do you need a break?

- How are you feeling?

Be honest with yourself.

Self-confidence is the best outfit.

When at its best, glowing and blemish-free, skin makes all the difference to self-esteem.

As the largest organ in the body, skin should be tended carefully, gently and with understanding.

How to care for your skin

1. Apply factor 30+ sunscreen every day. Yes, every day.

2. Don't smoke (this really does apply to all aspects of wellness).

3. Understand your skin. Is it dry or oily or combination? Use products that match your skin type.

4. Don't scrub your skin – it causes existing conditions to flare up.

5. Gently cleanse your face twice a day and after sweating.

AMERICAN ACADEMY OF DERMATOLOGY

Great skin doesn't happen by chance,
it happens by appointment .

Lebanese rose water

Rose water and rose oil have long been associated with improving and plumping skin. Follow the Middle Eastern and particularly Lebanese tradition of drinking white tea – a mixture of hot water and rose water. Owing to its antioxidants, rose water is said to reduce inflammation, acne and wrinkles.

White teas all round, please.

Give your skin a treat

The silk dress that's always lurking unworn at the back of the wardrobe... bring it out and wear it. Appreciate how the fabric feels against your skin. Revel in the sense of luxury that fine fabrics bring to your body.

Climate and propriety dictate that we spend most of our lives clothed, but allowing your naked skin to experience the elements naturally can be most exhilarating.

Get comfortable

- Don't put yourself down
- Take care of your body
- Remind yourself what is important

Stroke a puppy

Stroking dogs and cats has been proven to release all the happy hormones, including serotonin, prolactin and oxytocin, necessary to help reduce blood pressure and flood our bodies with feelings of pleasure.

"Animals are such agreeable friends; they ask no questions, they pass no criticisms."

GEORGE ELIOT

German hydrotherapy

Bavarian priest, Sebastian Kneipp, pioneered natural water therapy along the River Danube in the 19th century. Known as Kneipp Therapy, the hot and cold contrast water therapies, as practised in the German spa tradition, are going global.

Look out for hot and cold wading pools coming to a spa near you. Be like the Bavarians and enjoy the shock of cold water and the soothing properties of hot water to stimulate blood circulation, healthy complexions and energized immune systems.

Unwind

There is nothing quite like a bubble bath to arouse feelings of relaxation, calm and indulgence...

- Light candles
- Turn on soothing music
- Lock the door
- Let the water and bubbles flow
- Ahh

"Sorrow can be alleviated by good sleep, a bath and a glass of wine."

THOMAS AQUINAS

Hungarian thermal spa treatments

With over 1,000 thermal springs, Hungary is the thermal spa capital of Europe. Hungarians head to their local baths for camaraderie as much as health. Rich in minerals, "taking the waters" is said to ease joint pain and help soothe skin conditions. It's also just lovely and relaxing. To recreate the Hungarian spa experience at home, add magnesium salt to your tub, sit back and let nature do the rest.

How to make a mineral bath worthy of the finest spa:

- 250g (9oz) of Epsom salt or magnesium flakes

- 130g (4½oz) Himalayan pink salt

- ½ tsp of natural vanilla extract

- 10–15 drops of essential oil of your choice

Treat yourself

If time and finances allow, enjoying a massage is probably the finest way to hit your self-care high. Oiled hands pummelling taut muscles and soothing music washing over you provides powerful stress relief.

Reasons to get a massage:

- Relaxation
- Stress relief
- Fitness maintenance
- Reduction of pain
- Flexibility

Remember the three Rs

- Relax
- Refresh
- Recharge

Turkish *hammam*

Turkish women have perfected the art of the spa. Integral to community life, the Turkish spa or *hammam* provides not only bathing and massage facilities but all manner of beauty treatments.

Turkish women also celebrate life's milestones at the hammam, including "bridal bath" ceremonies one day before wedding festivities commence, post-birth bathing ceremonies, "tear-drying baths" after someone has died, "votary baths" after someone's wish has been fulfilled, "guest baths" to share with guests and "holiday baths" to prepare for religious holidays.

"Hair is everything."

PHOEBE WALLER-BRIDGE

Bad hair has nowhere to hide – not even under a hat as that just makes it worse.

Good hair = good day

(Don't let anyone tell you otherwise)

Rub a tiny amount of argan oil on your palms and through your hair for extra shine.

Three golden rules for good hair:

1. Find a hairdresser you trust and who knows and loves your hair.

2. Go to said hairdresser regularly.

3. Eat omega-3 fatty acids for glossy hair (avocados, oily fish and pumpkin seeds, for instance).

Love is in the (h)air.

Personal care

Keeping your intimate parts clean is essential. Remember that all bodies are different, but here are some general top tips:

- Clean daily
- Use unperfumed soaps
- Do regular exercise
- Eat a balanced diet
- Wear comfortable underwear (preferably cotton)

It is estimated that women have an average of 500 periods in their lifetime... as if we haven't got enough on.

That women undergo this major bodily change month in month out is miraculous, and when understood properly, periods need not negatively affect daily life.

- **Monitor your cycle**
  Recognize when to expect any pre- or post-menstrual symptoms and when to anticipate bleeding. This will allow you to take charge of your period.

- **Keep a period journal**
  Understand how oestrogen and progesterone hormones affect your body and mood.

- **Eat dark chocolate during your period**
  The magnesium contained in cacao can help alleviate cramps.

- **Work with your body**
  Sure, some advertising suggests that menstruating women love nothing more than going skydiving, but don't be afraid to say, "Actually no thanks, I've got my period and I'm off to bed with a hot-water bottle."

Menstruation health needs to be taken seriously – bad periods can significantly influence your wellbeing (not just your laundry).

How to treat period pain

- Stopping smoking
- Exercise
- Heat (a hot-water bottle or heat pad)
- Warm bath or shower
- Massage
- Relaxation techniques

UK NATIONAL HEALTH SERVICE

Pay attention to your sensuality

With or without a partner, masturbation is an activity that has zero negative effects. Instead, exploring your body and bringing yourself to orgasm releases endorphins and thus floods your body with feelings of happiness. Understanding what stimulates your body also improves your sex life, relieves tension and helps you to sleep better.

Sexual activity is proven to reduce stress, improve mental health and decrease muscle tension.

Stand up tall.

Posture

Maintaining good posture will allow you to work more efficiently with less strain on your joints and ligaments. Good posture gives your whole body balance and reduces the chance of injury when exercising.

> *"A good stance and posture reflect a proper state of mind."*

MORIHEI UESHIBA

Self-care: the basics #5

Mastering good posture can help maintain bone and joint health and prevent pain and future back issues. It also makes you look more presentable and approachable.

How to stand properly:

1. Bear your weight primarily on the balls of your feet.

2. Keep your knees slightly bent.

3. Keep your feet about shoulder-width apart.

4. Let your arms hang naturally down the sides of the body.

5. Stand straight and tall with your shoulders pulled backward.

6. Tuck your stomach in.

7. Keep your head level.

THE AMERICAN CHIROPRACTIC ASSOCIATION

Adore your core.

With about 100 trillion bacteria, good and bad, living in your gut, the gut microbiota is increasingly seen as vital to good health.

How to have a happy gut

1. Lower stress levels to calm the nerves in your tummy.

2. Prioritize getting between seven and nine hours of sleep each night to give your gut enough time to digest and reset.

3. Eat slowly to enable your body to absorb nutrients and promote good digestion.

4. Take a walk after eating.

Good for your gut

- Sauerkraut
- Miso
- Natural yoghurt
- Garlic
- Onion
- Sourdough bread
- Almonds
- Olive oil

Bulgarian yoghurt

Bulgaria is one of the countries with the largest number of people living to be over 100. Its thick, unctuous, fatty yoghurt is believed to be one of the principal causes of such longevity. Bulgarian yoghurt teems with *Lactobacillus bulgaricus* probiotic "good bacteria" that promotes digestive health and boosts the immune system, and is eaten with almost every meal in Bulgaria. Bulgarian yoghurt starter kits can be bought over the internet and the yoghurt easily made in your own kitchen.

Remember you have two hands, one for helping others and the other for helping yourself.

Reach out to those you love. Make sure you hug your loved ones at least once a day.

Need to calm down quickly?

Stand up and place your arms high above your head. Count slowly to 20. Feel your pulse slow. Relax your arms and continue, refreshed and centred.

Keep hold

It's too easy to forget all the lovely things that people say. Make sure you keep hold of cards from loved ones and read them back for a little pick-me-up when you need it.

Write a to-do list every day and make sure you put your wellbeing at the top.

Focus, focus, focus...
on looking after yourself

- Book that doctor's appointment

- Make time for friends, family and yourself

- Complete your to-do list and reward yourself with a treat

Let it go

Nothing is as draining to mental and physical health than carrying around old grudges and hostilities. For instant lift, let them go.

....No?

You still think the argument is worth winning?

You are still convinced that they should apologize?

Drop it. Forgive. Wave goodbye to resentment and anger, and move on.

You will find yourself happier to have shaken off that horrible stretch of negativity.

Order your life in such a way that you are in control of it, and not it in control of you.

Brazilian nail polish

For most Brazilian women, it is inconceivable that they would not apply nail polish at least once a week. Brazilian manicures have the added bonus of being "messy", with polish covering not only the nail but also the skin surrounding the nail. This is then cleaned up to leave a longer-lasting polish.

With the ubiquity of nail bars on all high streets, getting your nails done is an instant way to achieve a glamorous beauty high.

Say yes to manicures –
if only for the health benefits

Manicures not only make your hands and nails look pretty but are also a great way to destress.

*"I believe in manicures.
I believe in overdressing.
I believe in primping at
leisure and wearing lipstick."*

AUDREY HEPBURN

For the softest of hands, slather with hand cream before bedtime and wear 100% cotton gloves while sleeping.

Love yourself.

"If you can't love yourself, how in the hell you gonna love somebody else?"

RUPAUL

Fall in love with yourself,
mind, body and soul.

"There is no charm equal to tenderness of heart."

JANE AUSTEN

Falling in love with yourself
doesn't make you vain, it
makes you indestructible.

Spend quality time with...

- People you love
- People who make you happy
- People you miss
- Yourself

Nothing nourishes us like good-quality relationships. Humans are social animals after all. Laughing with friends is vital to good health: it relieves stress and reminds us of the joys of being alive.

Be proactive in maintaining friendships:

- Suggest things to do together
- If friends can't make it, be persistent in rearranging
- Call just for a chat
- Arrange evenings in or trips away

Expecting other people to provide the fun will always lead to disappointment.

"What does love look like? It has the hands to help others. It has the feet to hasten to the poor and needy. It has eyes to see misery and want. It has the ears to hear the sighs and sorrows of men. That is what love looks like."

SAINT AUGUSTINE

The incredible thing about love is that there is always more of it: the more you give, the more you will receive.

"Being deeply loved by someone gives you strength, while loving someone deeply gives you courage."

LAO TZU

Say "*I love you*"
to yourself.

Say "*I love you*"
to your lover and family.

Say "*I love you*"
at the close of every day.

*" If you look into your own heart,
and you find nothing wrong there,
what is there to worry about?
What is there to fear?"*

CONFUCIUS

We don't all need to run marathons to keep a healthy heart, rather we simply need activities that will make us:

- Breathe harder
- Feel warmer
- Get our hearts to beat faster

Learning to care for yourself is
the foundation to everything –
it is the only way to stand tall.

Move like you love yourself.

Keep moving

If you're seeking to exercise more, aim to be active for 2½–5 hours per week, taking up activities such as:

- Fast walking
- Jogging
- Swimming
- Tennis

UK NATIONAL HEALTH SERVICE

Avoid setting unachievable goals such as pumping weights at the gym *every* night until you're a lean, mean fighting machine. Instead, incorporate manageable exercise into your daily routine. Think about your schedule and weave in exercise that works for you.

Once exercise becomes a habit, it is then no longer a chore.

"Be sure you put your feet in the right place, then stand firm."

ABRAHAM LINCOLN

Norwegian *friluftsliv*

Be like the Norwegians and immerse yourself in nature. *Friluftsliv* (pronounced free-loofts-liv) refers to the idea of open-air living or free air life. Norwegian companies encourage their staff to take afternoons off to walk or trek outside. Hearty outdoor activities can range from kayaking to campfires, and it's believed that spending time outside enhances fitness and friendships, and brings a fresh burst of stability to your life. So plan your *friluftsliv* weekend as soon as possible!

Studies conducted by King's College London using the Urban Mind app have demonstrated that being exposed to nature, going for a walk, gardening or having a run in the countryside benefits the individual for up to seven hours after the experience.

"There are moments when all anxiety and stated toil are becalmed in the infinite leisure and repose of nature."

HENRY DAVID THOREAU

Shinrin-yoku Japanese forest bathing

Shinrin-yoku or forest bathing is seen to be so important to overall wellness that it is formally encouraged by the Japanese government. People in Japan are urged to spend time in woodlands, not exercising but simply walking or being close to trees.

Tackling both mental and physical health, forest bathing is an easy and free method of seeking a calmer, more centred sense of self.

One theory behind the efficacy of forest bathing relates to how trees release phytoncides. These essential oils are emitted to protect trees from germs and insects, and are believed to improve people's immunity.

How to forest bathe
in urban environments

If there is no forest or woodland near you, there is robust evidence to suggest that spending time in any green space has significant health benefits.

- Find your nearest green space and commit to spending at least 30 minutes a day awash with fresh air.

- Be brave and hug a tree. For a good dose of phytoncides, the woodland essential oils that are said to improve immunity, get up close and breathe in.

- Choose a desk that has views over trees rather than an urban view.

- If actual woodland or trees are impossible to access, buy some nature-inspired artwork and hang it where you will see it frequently.

QUOTES ARE TAKEN FROM

Abraham Lincoln: 19th-century US President

Albert Einstein: 20th-century physicist and all-round genius

Audrey Hepburn: 20th-century film star

Confucius: Ancient Chinese philosopher and politician

Earl Nightingale: 20th-century American author

George Eliot: 19th-century English author of *Middlemarch*

Henry David Thoreau: 19th-century American essayist

Jane Austen: 19th-century English author of *Pride and Prejudice*

John Lubbock: 19th-century English philanthropist

Lao Tzu: Ancient Chinese philosopher

Lord Byron: 19th-century English Romantic poet

Marcel Proust: 20th-century French author of *In Search of Lost Time*

Mark Twain: 19th-century American author of *Huckleberry Finn* and *Tom Sawyer*

Mary J. Blige: 20th-century American singer and songwriter

Morihei Ueshiba: Japanese martial artist and founder of aikido

Phoebe Waller-Bridge: 21st-century actress and writer of television comedy-drama series *Fleabag*

Plato: Ancient Greek philosopher

RuPaul: American drag queen and TV personality

Saint Augustine: 1st-century Roman African theologian

Sophia Loren: 20th-century film star

Thomas Aquinas: 13thcentury Italian theologian

BOOKS AND FURTHER READING

Beyond Happiness by Anthony Seldon,
Yellow Kite

Herbal Remedies Handbook by Andrew
Chevallier, DK

The Holy Bible, English Standard Version

*Ikigai: The Japanese Secret to a Long and Happy
Life,* by Héctor García, Hutchinson

Neal's Yard Remedies Complete Wellness, DK

Oxford Dictionary of Quotations, Oxford University Press

The Good Gut: Taking Control of Your Weight, Your Mood, and Your Long Term Health by Justin Sonnenburg and Erica Sonnenburg, Penguin

The Happy Kitchen: Good Mood Food by Rachel Kelly and Alice Mackintosh, Short Books

The Things You Can See Only When You Slow Down: How to be Calm in a Busy World by Haemin Sunim, Penguin

USEFUL WEBSITES

aad.org

acatoday.org

bacillusbulgaricus.com

college-optometrists.org

developinggoodhabits.com

eufic.org

germany.travel

internationalliving.com

mind.org.uk

natureandforesttherapy.org

nhs.org.uk

psychologytoday.com

sweden.se

tinybuddha.com

turkishculture.org

urbanmind.info

visit-hungary.com

wellandgood.com

worldatlas.com

visitnorway.com

Publishing Director Sarah Lavelle
Editor Harriet Webster
Assistant Editor Stacey Cleworth
Words Joanna Gray
Series Designer Emily Lapworth
Junior Designer Alicia House
Production Director Stephen Lang
Production Controller Sinead Hering

Published in 2019 by Quadrille,
an imprint of Hardie Grant
Publishing

Quadrille
52–54 Southwark Street
London SE1 1UN
quadrille.com

The publisher has made every
effort to trace the copyright
holders. We apologize in advance
for any unintentional omissions
and would be pleased to insert the
appropriate acknowledgement in
any subsequent edition.

Cataloguing in Publication Data:
a catalogue record for this book is
available from the British Library.

ISBN 978 1 78713 517 8

Printed in China